LET'S EXPLORE LIFE SCIENCE

Exploring

FOOD AND NUTRITION

Ella Hawley

PowerKiDS
press.

New York

Published in 2013 by The Rosen Publishing Group, Inc.
29 East 21st Street, New York, NY 10010

First Edition

Editor: Jennifer Way
Book Design: Kate Laczynski

Photo Credits: Cover © www.iStockphoto.com/Francisco Romero; cover (background) © www.iStockphoto.com/M. Eric Honeycutt; cover (pepper, orange) PhotoDisc; pp. 4–5, 6 (milk, cheese), 7, 9 (left, right), 10–11, 11 (right), 13, 16, 17, 19, 20–21, 22 Shutterstock.com; p. 8 AbleStock.com/Thinkstock; p. 12 Jupiterimages/Pixland/Thinkstock; p. 15 (fruit) © www.iStockphoto.com/Morgan Lane Studios; p. 15 (grains) © www.iStockphoto.com/Ferhat Mat; p. 15 (milk) © www.iStockphoto.com/AjFilGud; p. 15 (meat) © www.iStockphoto.com/Jack Puccio; p. 15 (vegetables) © www.iStockphoto.com/Maria Toutoudaki; p. 18 © www.iStockphoto.com/Skip O'Donnell.

Library of Congress Cataloging-in-Publication Data

Hawley, Ella.
  Exploring food and nutrition / by Ella Hawley. — 1st ed.
    p. cm. — (Let's explore life science)
  Includes index.
  ISBN 978-1-4488-6176-7 (library binding) — ISBN 978-1-4488-6310-5 (pbk.) — ISBN 978-1-4488-6311-2 (6-pack)
  1. Nutrition—Juvenile literature. 2. Food—Juvenile literature. I. Title.
  RA784.H376 2013
  613.2—dc23
                                    2011027688

Manufactured in the United States of America

CPSIA Compliance Information: Batch #SW12PK: For Further Information contact Rosen Publishing, New York, New York at 1-800-237-9932

CONTENTS

Food Is Important!

You may think you know a lot about food because you eat it every day. However, the food you eat is more important than you might realize. Food gives your body the energy and **nutrients** it needs to be healthy and strong.

All the different kinds of foods you eat is called your diet. When you pick unhealthy things to eat, it makes your body less healthy. Over time, it can even make you sick. Unhealthy foods include those foods that are high in sugars and fats. Healthy foods include vegetables, fruits, whole grains, and proteins. Are you ready to find out more about food and nutrition?

Choosing to eat a variety of fruits, vegetables, whole grains, and proteins gives you a balanced diet. It can be easier and more fun to do this if the people you eat with most often share this goal.

What Are Nutrients?

Did you know that each food gives your body certain nutrients? For example, a glass of milk gives your body calcium, which is a nutrient that makes your bones strong and healthy.

Nutrients are the things in food that your body uses to do different jobs. The muscles use some nutrients. The brain and the blood use others. Nutrients give your body

Milk, cheese, and other dairy products contain calcium, as well as nutrients such as vitamin D.

energy, too. Food energy is measured in **calories**. If you eat more calories than your body can use up, or burn, then your body stores these calories as fat.

Getting the right balance of nutrients keeps you strong and healthy. You would not be able to go for a hike without the energy you get from nutrients!

Grains and Proteins

One of the main food groups we need to eat from is the grains group. Bread, pasta, and oatmeal are grain products. Grains have **carbohydrates**, which give the body energy.

Foods can be made from whole grains or **refined** grains. Whole grains are healthier. Foods made with whole grains are made with the entire grain. Refined

Most pasta is made from wheat and comes in many shapes. Many types of pasta are made with refined grains, but the more nutritious whole-grain pastas are becoming more popular.

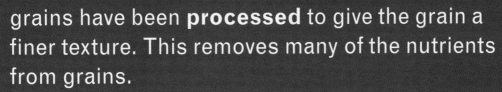

grains have been **processed** to give the grain a finer texture. This removes many of the nutrients from grains.

Proteins are another important food group. They are the building blocks of your muscles, organs, and other bodily tissues. Meat, poultry, fish, nuts, beans, and eggs are some foods we eat to get protein.

Some protein-rich foods also have a lot of fat. It is a good idea to pick lean proteins, like grilled chicken, which are low in fat.

There are lots of different kinds of beans. Beans are a good source of protein, especially for people who want to eat less meat or for vegetarians. Vegetarians are people who do not eat meat.

Vitamins and Minerals

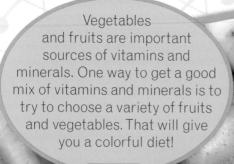

Vegetables and fruits are important sources of vitamins and minerals. One way to get a good mix of vitamins and minerals is to try to choose a variety of fruits and vegetables. That will give you a colorful diet!

Vitamins and minerals make our bodies work as they should. Some vitamins, such as vitamins A, D, E, and K, can be stored in your body when you do not use them up. Some vitamins cannot be stored, so you need to eat foods with these

vitamins every day. Vitamins C and B are vitamins that cannot be stored.

Minerals come from the soil or water and are taken in by plants and animals. Calcium is an important mineral. Iron, zinc, and copper are a few other minerals we need in small amounts.

People take vitamin pills to supplement their diets. "To supplement" means "to make up for something that is missing." Doctors think that while most vitamin pills will not hurt you, it is best to get your nutrients from food.

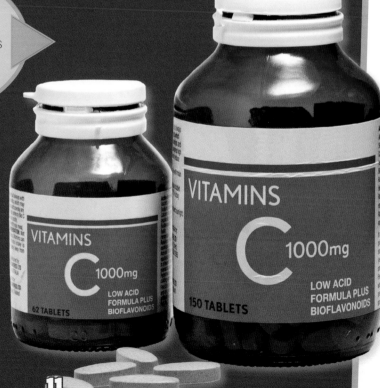

Fat, Fiber, and Water

The vitamins and minerals found in healthy foods are all important. Water is important, too. Water helps the body do many jobs. It is part of your blood, your **digestive juices**, and your waste.

Unlike water, fat is something we need only a small amount of. Your body needs fat to heal its cells. Fat is important for young children, too. It

Drinking water is another part of a healthy diet. Water makes up more than half of your body's composition!

Oatmeal is a good source of fiber. Fiber helps you feel full faster and stay full longer so you do not overeat.

helps the brain and central nervous system grow the way it should. Too much fat, though, can cause health problems.

Some foods have fiber in them. Whole grains, fruits, and vegetables are high in fiber. Fiber helps your body digest food.

MyPlate: A Guide for Healthy Eating

The U.S. Department of Agriculture created MyPlate as a guide for eating a healthy, **balanced** diet. The MyPlate chart shows how much of each food group we should be eating. It also shows that eating foods from all the food groups is important.

Fruits and vegetables should make up half of the food you eat each day. Grains are the next-biggest piece of the pie. Proteins make up a bit less than a quarter of your diet. Dairy products, such as milk, yogurt, and cheese, should be a part of each meal, too.

This graphic organizer shows how much of each type of food makes up a healthy diet. It is based on the USDA's MyPlate chart. Oils, fats, and sweets are not shown because they should be eaten only in small amounts.

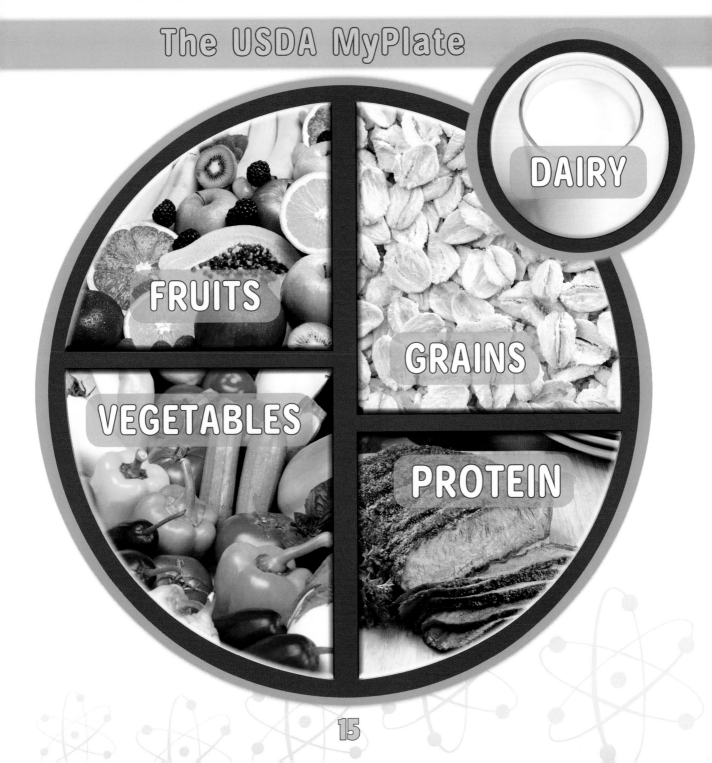

Read the Label

Market Pantry canned pasta combines quality

value in a rich and hearty home-style me...

Nutrition Facts
Serving Size 1 cup (252g)
Servings Per Container about 2

Amount Per Serving

Calories 270   Calories from Fat 70

	% Daily Value*
Total Fat 7g	**11%**
Saturated Fat 2.5g	**13%**
Trans Fat 0g	
Cholesterol 15mg	**5%**
Sodium 1310mg	**54%**
Total Carbohydrate 43g	**14%**
Dietary Fiber 2g	**6%**
Sugars 9g	
Protein 9g	

Vitamin A 10%	•	Vitamin C 0%	
Calcium 2%	•	Iron 10%	

* Percent Daily Values are based on a
2,000 calorie diet.

INGREDIENTS: WATER, TOM...
TER, TOMATO PASTE, EN...
FLOUR (WHEAT FLOUR, NIACIN, ...
MONONITRATE, RIBOFLAVIN, ...
BEEF, HIGH FRUCTOSE CORN SYR...
MEAL (WHEAT FLOUR, WATER, ...
CORN STARCH, SALT, TEXTURED ...
PROTEIN (SOY FLOUR, CARAMEL ...
URAL FLAVOR, SEASONING (HYDR...
LYZED CORN AND SOY ...
LYZED CORN GLUTE...
ONION POWDER, CITRIC ...
GLUTAMATE, CARAMEL COLOR), ...
FIED CHEESE (CHEDDAR ...
CHEESE CULTURES, SALT, EN...
SALT, DISODIUM PHOSPHATE), ...
RIKA, OLEORESIN CARDAMO... PAP...
CONTAINS: WHEAT, SOY, MILK

212 22 0137 I02061...

0 85239 221...

Along with a nutrition-facts chart, food labels have a list of ingredients. If there are lots of long words you cannot say, it might a good idea to put that food back on the shelf!

There are a lot of different foods to choose from at the supermarket. It can be hard to know which box of cereal or loaf of bread is the best one to buy.

Not all foods are created equal. It is a good habit to read the labels on food so that you know what is in it. Packaged foods in supermarkets have nutrition guides. These guides tell you how much one serving of that food is, how many calories it has, and how much fat, salt, protein, fiber, and other nutrients there are. Reading the labels can help you make better food choices.

Reading labels teaches you what is in the food you eat. They can help you avoid unhealthy foods and look for healthier options.

Processed Foods

People have been processing foods for much of human history. Processing a food means you change it so that you can eat it or so that you can store it longer than you could a fresh food. Baking a cake is one way of processing food. Smoking meats is another one.

Today, food companies have many other means of processing foods. They often add **chemicals** to food that keep it from spoiling. These modern processes make it possible to buy food in **bulk** and store it. This food is often less costly than fresh food. Often it is also less healthy.

Diet sodas and sugar-free or fat-free processed foods often have a long list of chemicals in them. While too much fat and sugar are not healthy, neither are these chemicals!

Food and Health

Diet can affect health in good ways or in bad ways. More than one-third of all American adults over age 20 are **obese**. One-fifth of all American children are obese, too! Obesity can lead to serious health problems such as **diabetes**, high blood pressure, and heart disease.

Around 25.8 million Americans have diabetes. The bodies of people with diabetes cannot break down sugars properly. This hurts the body, and can lead to blindness and kidney failure.

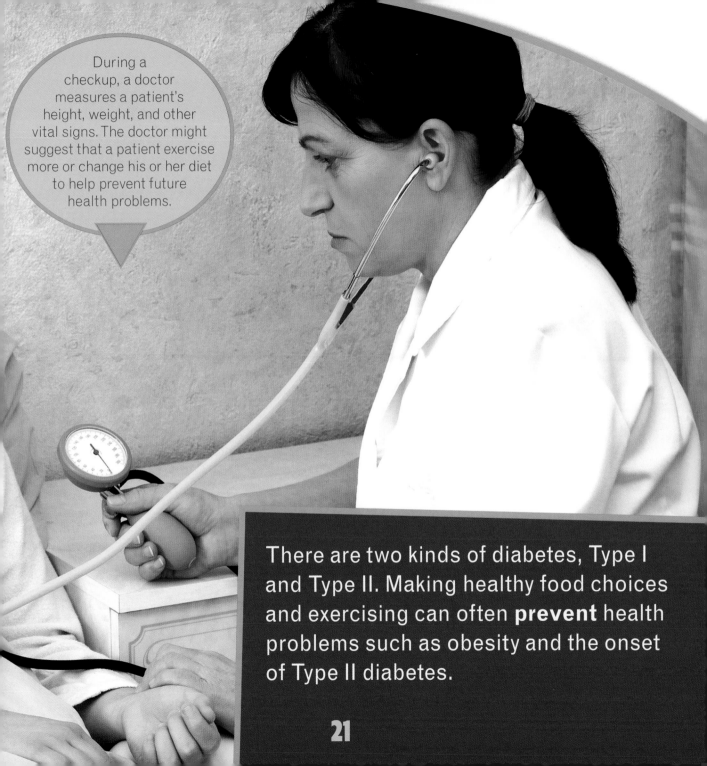

During a checkup, a doctor measures a patient's height, weight, and other vital signs. The doctor might suggest that a patient exercise more or change his or her diet to help prevent future health problems.

There are two kinds of diabetes, Type I and Type II. Making healthy food choices and exercising can often **prevent** health problems such as obesity and the onset of Type II diabetes.

21

Learning Healthy Habits

American nutrition is in trouble. There are so many foods on the grocery store shelves that we are being flooded with choices. Many of these foods are unhealthy. The government and other groups are trying to teach people about healthy foods, balanced nutrition, and how to read food labels.

Making exercise a part of your life is important, and it can be fun, too!

Even with education, the battle for a healthy nation is not over. Many people live in food deserts. They may live far away from stores that sell healthy foods, or healthy foods may be too costly for them. The government is working on solving this problem. What changes can you make to be healthier?

GLOSSARY

balanced (BAL-ensd) Having the right mix of things.

bulk (BULK) A large amount.

calories (KA-luh-reez) Amounts of food that the body uses to keep working.

carbohydrates (kar-boh-HY-drayts) The main element in foods made mostly from plants, such as potatoes and bread.

chemicals (KEH-mih-kulz) Matter that can be mixed with other matter to cause changes.

diabetes (dy-uh-BEE-teez) A sickness in which a person's body cannot take in sugar and starch normally.

digestive juices (dy-JES-tiv JOOS-ez) Matter in the body that helps break down food into energy.

nutrients (NOO-tree-ents) Food that a living thing needs to live and grow.

obese (oh-BEES) Having too much body fat.

prevent (prih-VENT) To keep something from happening.

processed (PRAH-sesd) Changed by a set of actions.

refined (rih-FYND) Purified through mechanical or chemical processes.

INDEX

WEB SITES

Due to the changing nature of Internet links, PowerKids Press has developed an online list of Web sites related to the subject of this book. This site is updated regularly. Please use this link to access the list:
www.powerkidslinks.com/lels/food/